1·2·3 Draw
CARTOON FACES

A step-by-step guide

by Steve Barr

PEEL PRODUCTIONS, INC.

This book is dedicated to my
brothers and sisters: Laurie and
Gregg, who always make me
smile; Rob and Cindy, who
always make me laugh; and Tim,
who keeps me humble.

—S.B.

Published by Peel Productions, Inc.
Printed in China

Library of Congress Cataloging-in-Publication Data

Barr, Steve, 1958-
  1-2-3 draw cartoon faces : a step-by-step guide / by Steve
Barr.
    p. cm.
  Contents: Basic shapes and lines -- Boy's face -- Girl's face -- Man's face --
Grandfather's face -- Grandmother's face -- Talking lady -- Eyes -- Hair --
Emotions -- Hats -- Glasses.
    ISBN 0-939217-47-3 (alk. paper)
  1. Face--Caricatures and cartoons--Juvenile literature. 2. Cartooning--
Technique--Juvenile literature. [1. Cartooning--Technique. 2. Drawing--
Technique. 3. Face in art.] I. Title. II. Title: Faces. III. Title: One-two-three draw
cartoon faces.
  NC1764.8.F33B37 2002
  741.5--dc21
                        2002009925

Distributed to the trade and art
markets in North America by

NORTH LIGHT BOOKS,
an imprint of F&W Publications, Inc.
4700 East Galbraith Road
Cincinnati, OH 45236

(800) 289-0963

Contents

Before you begin...

Stop! Look! Listen!

You will need:

1. a sharpened pencil
2. paper
3. an eraser
4. a pencil sharpener
5. colored pencils, markers or crayons
6. a comfortable place to sit and draw
7. a good light source

Let's draw cartoon faces!

No Rules!

This book is designed to teach the basics of drawing cartoon faces. There are no rules about cartooning, so you can spend hours sketching, doodling and playing with different lines and shapes.

Sketch, doodle, play!

If the instructions tell you to use an oval to draw a nose and you want to use a triangle, draw a triangle. Cartooning is all about having fun drawing. Explore, experiment with crazy ideas. If it makes you smile and makes your friends giggle, you're doing it right!

Cartooning tips:

1 Draw lightly at first—SKETCH, so you can erase extra lines easily.

2 Practice, practice, practice!

3 Have fun cartooning!

Basic Shapes and Lines

Here are basic shapes and lines you will use to draw cartoon faces:

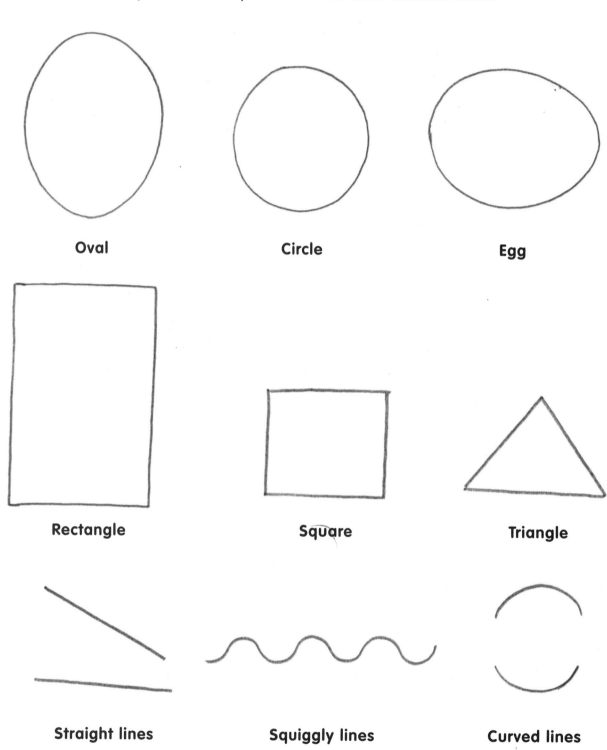

Oval

Circle

Egg

Rectangle

Square

Triangle

Straight lines

Squiggly lines

Curved lines

Boy's Face

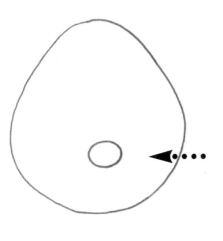

Let's begin by using some of the basic shapes and lines to draw a boy's face.

1 Sketch a large **oval** for the head, with a smaller **oval** inside it for the nose.

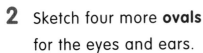

2 Sketch four more **ovals** for the eyes and ears.

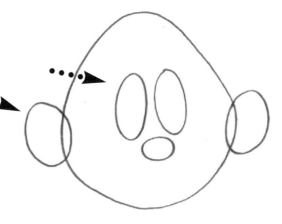

3 Sketch a big **oval** on the top for hair. Draw two **circles** inside each eye.

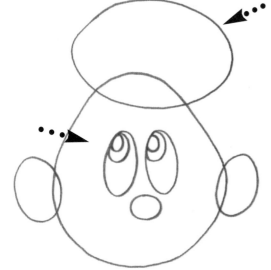

4 Add a **curved line** on each side to make more hair. Darken around the top circle of the eye.

7

5 Draw two small **triangles** for eyebrows. Sketch a small **curved line** for the mouth.

6 Darken the eyebrows. Put a small **line** on the end of the mouth.

7 LOOK at the final drawing! Erase the extra sketch lines. Darken the final lines. Add color.

Nice job!

Girl's Face

Let's draw a girl's face using more of the simple shapes and lines.

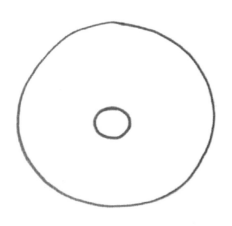

1 Sketch a **circle** with a small **circle** in the center.

2 Add small **ovals** for eyes. Draw a **curved line** for the mouth.

3 Draw small **ovals** inside the eyes. Add a small **curved line** on each end of the mouth.

4 Sketch two **curved lines** for hair. Darken part of the eyes. Draw L-shaped **lines** for the neck and shoulders.

5 Draw two long **curved lines**, meeting in the middle, for the hair. Draw **straight lines** for the bottom of the hair line.

6 Draw a few **triangles** to make the jagged ends of her hair.

7 LOOK at the final drawing! Erase the extra sketch lines. Add color.

Great girl's face!

Man's Face

Let's draw a father for the boy and girl.

1 This time, sketch a squashed **oval**, the shape of a kidney bean.

2 Sketch two **ovals**, for the nose and ear.

3 Draw two **ovals**, one inside the other, for each eye. Draw a **circle** inside the ear.

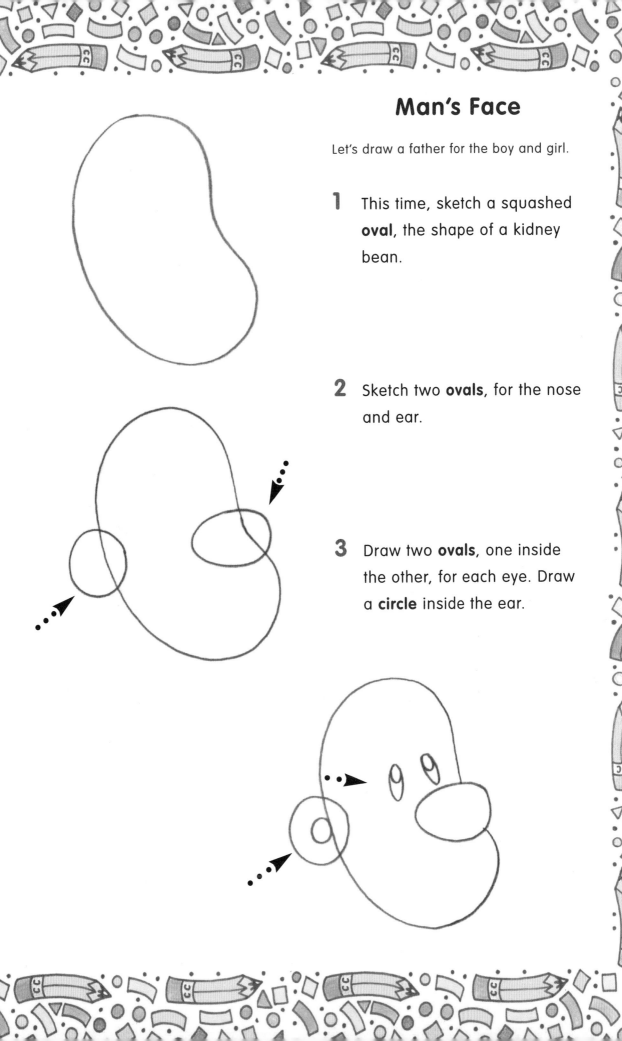

4 Sketch an **oval**, above the ear, for hair. Sketch two **rectangles**, above the eyes, for eyebrows.

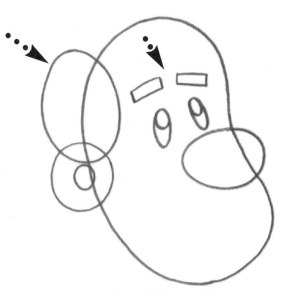

5 Sketch an **oval** on top and a **curved line** on the side, for more hair. Darken the eyebrows and part of each eye. Draw two **curved lines** for his mouth.

6 LOOK at the final drawing! Erase extra sketch lines. Add color.

Fabulous father!

Woman's Face

Let's draw a mom for the cartoon kids.

1 Draw another kidney bean shape—a squashed **oval**.

2 Sketch two **ovals**, for the eye and nose.

3 Sketch two overlapping **ovals** for hair. Draw two partial **ovals** inside her eye. Draw two **curved lines** for her mouth.

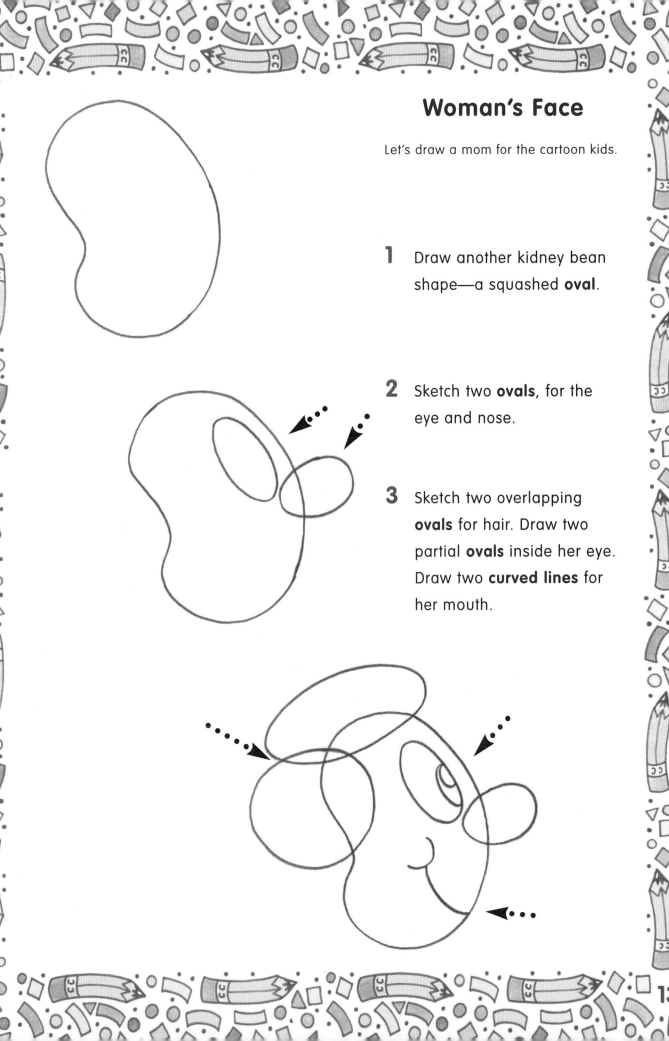

4 Sketch another overlapping oval to complete her hair.

5 Darken part of the eye. Draw three **straight lines** for eyelashes.

6 LOOK at the final drawing! Erase extra sketch lines. Color your cartoon mom's face any way you choose.

Wow! You've drawn a cartoon family! Good job!

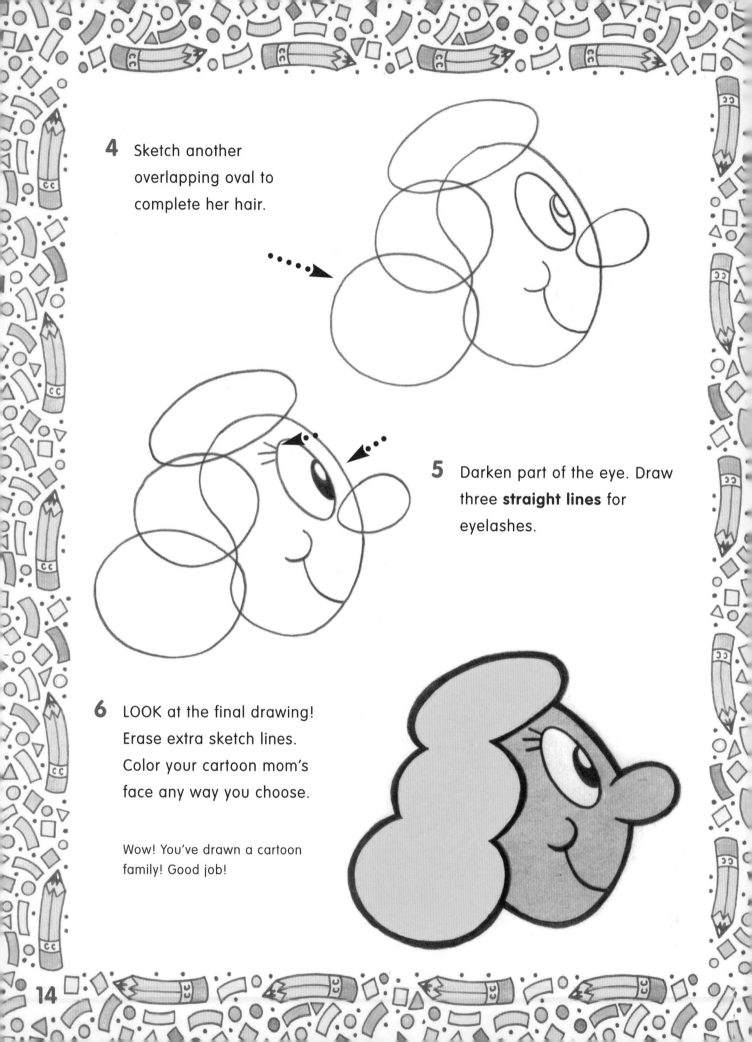

Grandpop's Face

Let's add to this family and draw cartoon grandparents. We'll begin with a grandpop.

1 Sketch a large **oval** for his head. Sketch two, overlapping **ovals** for his ear and nose.

2 Draw two **ovals** for each eye—one inside the other. Draw a small **circle** inside the ear.

3 Sketch two tilted **ovals** for eyebrows. Darken part of each eye.

4 Sketch another partial **oval** for hair.

5 Sketch a long **oval** to begin a droopy moustache.

6 Sketch another long **oval** to complete his moustache. Draw two **curved lines** to make a smiling mouth.

7 LOOK at the final drawing! Erase extra sketch lines. Darken the final lines. Color your cartoon grandpop.

Marvelous moustache!

Grandmother's Face

Now let's draw the grandmother.

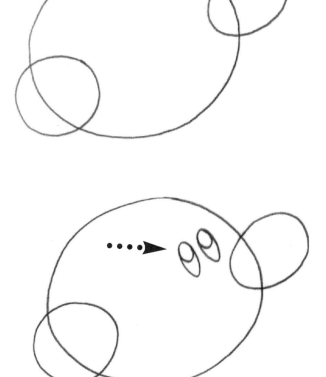

1 Sketch a large **oval** for her head and two smaller, overlapping **ovals** for the ear and nose.

2 Draw two **ovals** with small **circles** inside them for eyes.

3 Sketch an **oval** for hair. Add a **curved line** for her smiling mouth.

4 Sketch two more **ovals** for hair. Darken part of the eyes.

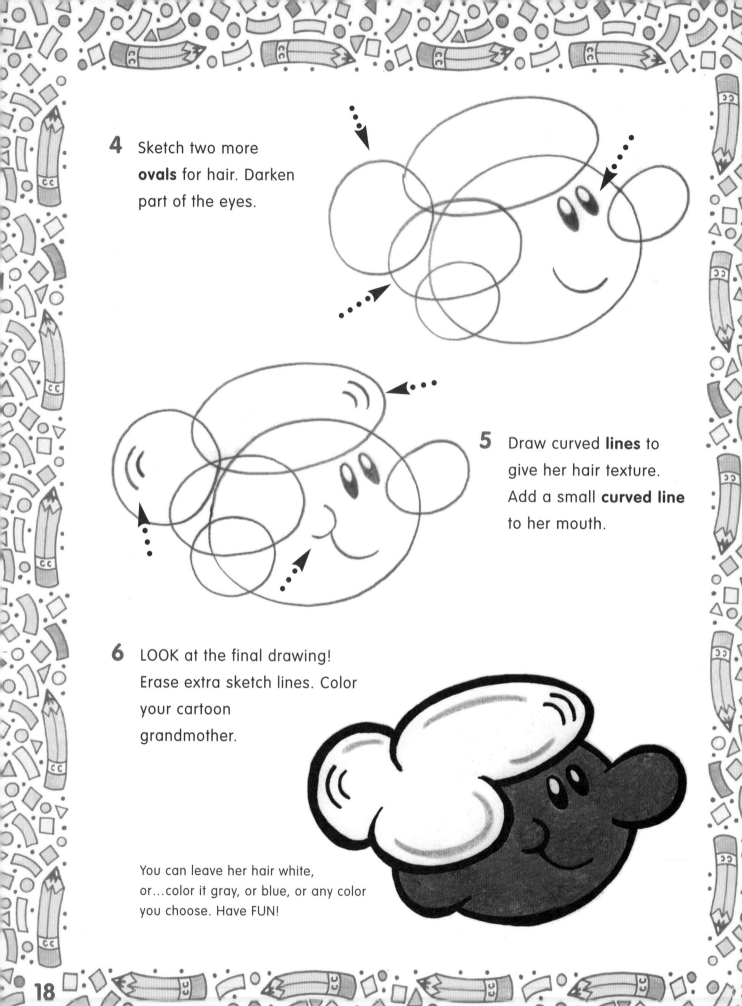

5 Draw curved **lines** to give her hair texture. Add a small **curved line** to her mouth.

6 LOOK at the final drawing! Erase extra sketch lines. Color your cartoon grandmother.

You can leave her hair white, or...color it gray, or blue, or any color you choose. Have FUN!

Hair

LOOK carefully at these drawings!
What looks the same in each drawing?
What is different in each drawing?

Each of the faces is identical. Only the hair has been changed. Isn't that incredible?

Hair can drastically change the way your cartoon face looks. Let's draw the same face and give him a different hairstyle.

1   Sketch three **ovals**: a large one for the head and two smaller ones for ears.

2   Draw a small **circle** inside each ear. Draw tilted **rectangles** for eyebrows. Draw a **circle** for the nose.

3   Draw two **ovals**, with **circles** inside them, for eyes. Draw a **curved line** for the mouth.

4   Darken around the eye circles. Add a small **curved lines** on each side of the mouth.

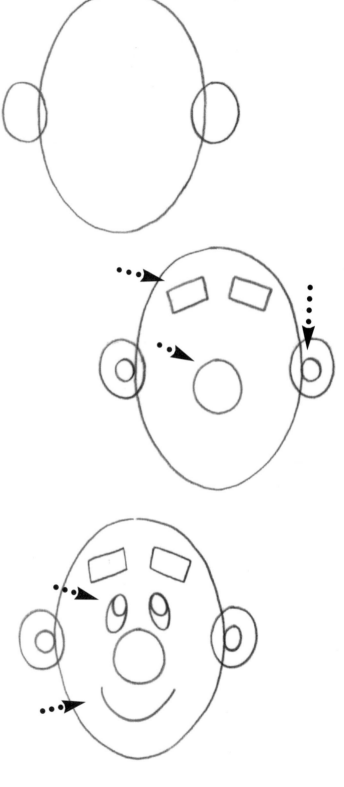

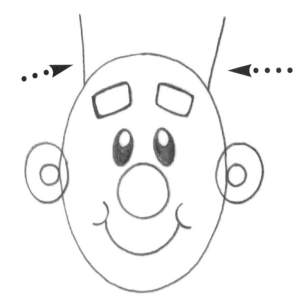

5 Draw two **straight lines** on the top of his head.

6 Connect them with a **squiggly line**. Add a small **curved line** across his forehead. Draw a few **straight lines** on each side of it for hair strands.

7 LOOK at the final drawing! Erase extra sketch lines. Add color.

Super crew cut! Is he in the military? Good Job!

Eyes

Using simple shapes, I will show you a few ways to draw cartoon eyes. You can learn a variety of ways to sketch cartoons by looking at cartoons in your newspaper or on television. Sketch what you see and experiment with some ideas of your own.

Simple black **circles** or **ovals** are easy to draw and make neat cartoon eyes!

Big **ovals** with white **ovals** inside black **ovals** make these big eyes. Lots of cartoonists use them on their cartoon characters. It looks like a little light is gleaming in the character's eyes.

If you add **curved lines** at the bottom of the big eyes, it gives your character puffy cheeks.

A **curved line** for one eye and one wide open eye make him look like he is winking.

You can make simple eyes with little **curved lines**. These, with a smile, make the character look happy.

Sketch these faces. Now sketch one with your favorite kind of eyes on it. Add color.

Expressions and Emotions

Using really simple shapes and lines, let's draw several different expressions showing emotions, on a basic cartoon face.

1 Sketch a large **oval** for the head and smaller **ovals** for ears.

2 Sketch an **oval** on top of the head for hair. Draw **ovals** for the eyes and nose.

3 Draw **curved lines** for more hair. Draw two more **ovals** inside each eye.

4 Darken part of the eyes.

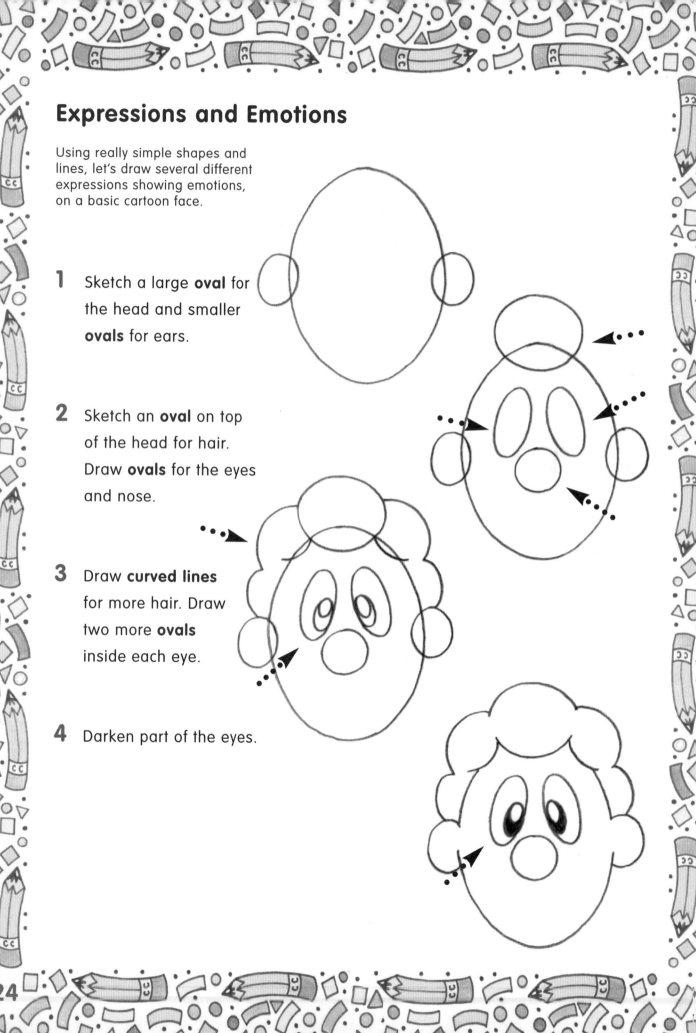

24

5 Add two **curved lines** for eyebrows and a big **curved line** for a mouth.

5 Draw two **straight lines** for eyebrows. Add an **oval** for his mouth.

LOOK at each of these faces! Can you see which lines and shapes make each drawing look different? Pick one of these and finish Step 5 of your drawing.

5 Draw two **curved lines** and an upside-down **curved line** for the mouth.

5 Draw two **straight lines** for eyebrows and a **curved lin**e for the mouth.

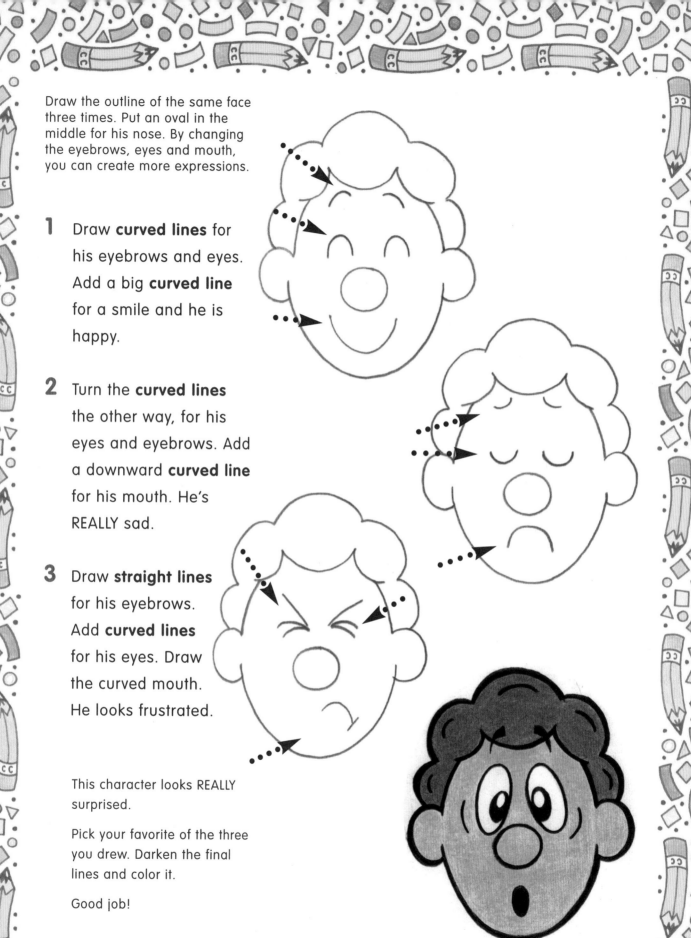

Draw the outline of the same face three times. Put an oval in the middle for his nose. By changing the eyebrows, eyes and mouth, you can create more expressions.

1 Draw **curved lines** for his eyebrows and eyes. Add a big **curved line** for a smile and he is happy.

2 Turn the **curved lines** the other way, for his eyes and eyebrows. Add a downward **curved line** for his mouth. He's REALLY sad.

3 Draw **straight lines** for his eyebrows. Add **curved lines** for his eyes. Draw the curved mouth. He looks frustrated.

This character looks REALLY surprised.

Pick your favorite of the three you drew. Darken the final lines and color it.

Good job!

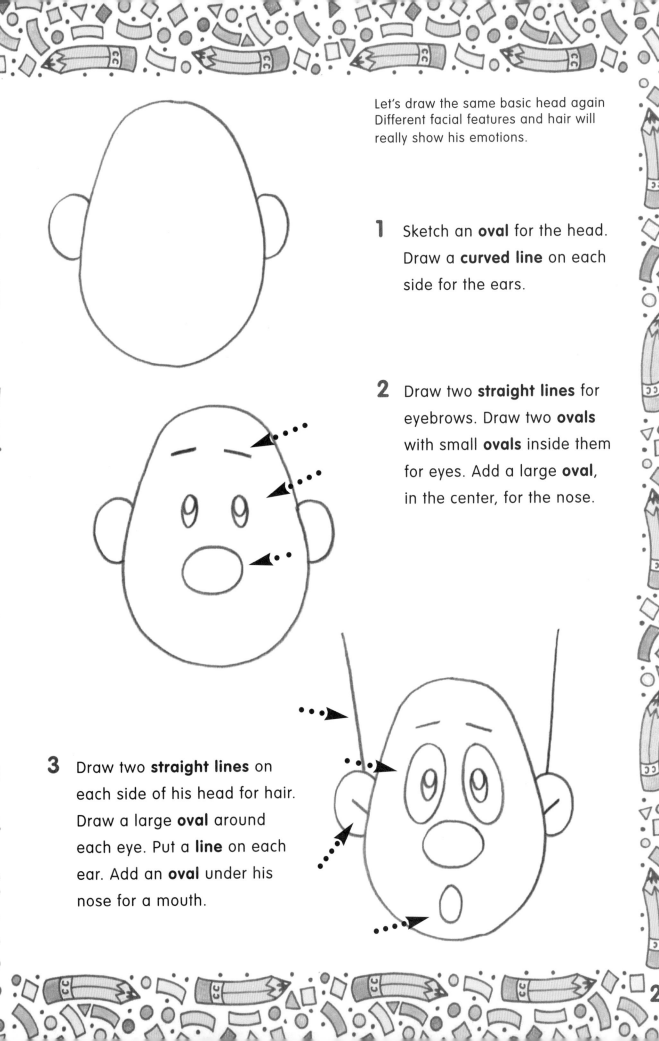

Let's draw the same basic head again. Different facial features and hair will really show his emotions.

1 Sketch an **oval** for the head. Draw a **curved line** on each side for the ears.

2 Draw two **straight lines** for eyebrows. Draw two **ovals** with small **ovals** inside them for eyes. Add a large **oval**, in the center, for the nose.

3 Draw two **straight lines** on each side of his head for hair. Draw a large **oval** around each eye. Put a **line** on each ear. Add an **oval** under his nose for a mouth.

4 Draw a small curved line on the top of his head. Darken part of the eyes and the mouth.

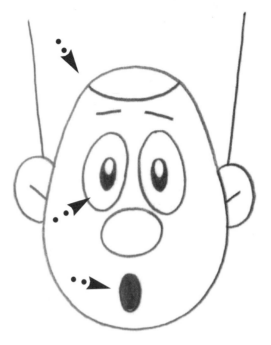

5 Draw a **squiggly line** for the top of his hair.

6 LOOK at the final drawing! Add color. He looks startled. Maybe he saw a ghost.

Maybe he's surprised at how well you drew him. His hair is standing on end!

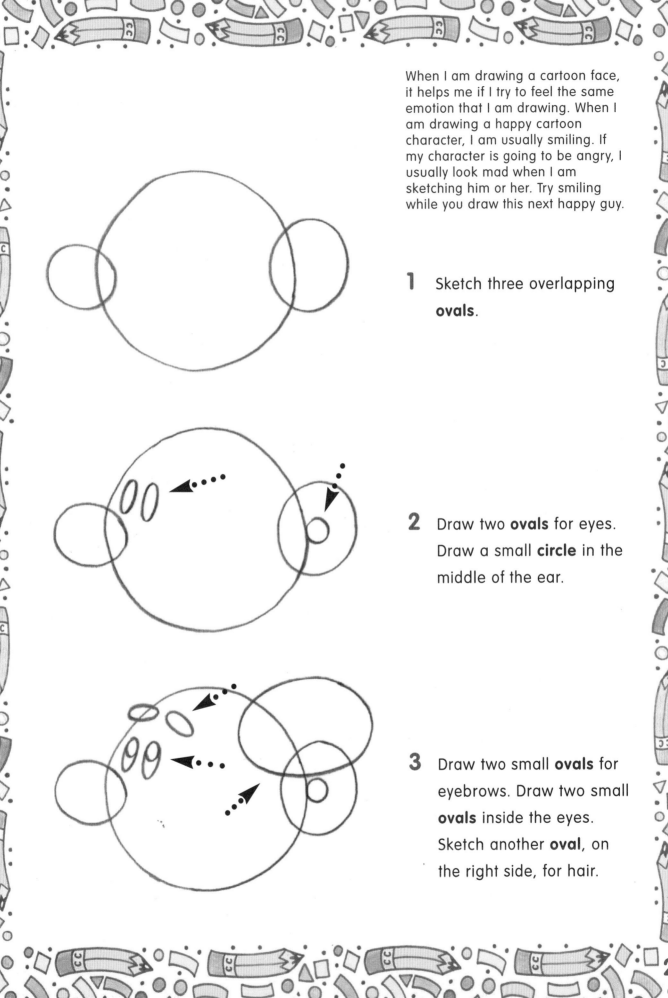

When I am drawing a cartoon face, it helps me if I try to feel the same emotion that I am drawing. When I am drawing a happy cartoon character, I am usually smiling. If my character is going to be angry, I usually look mad when I am sketching him or her. Try smiling while you draw this next happy guy.

1 Sketch three overlapping **ovals**.

2 Draw two **ovals** for eyes. Draw a small **circle** in the middle of the ear.

3 Draw two small **ovals** for eyebrows. Draw two small **ovals** inside the eyes. Sketch another **oval**, on the right side, for hair.

4 Darken the eyebrows and part of the eyes. Draw a **curved line** for a mouth, with a smaller **curved line** on the end of it to give him a cute cheek.

5 Draw **curved lines** that meet to make the wave shape for his hair. Add another **curved line** to his mouth.

6 Draw four **curved lines** in the wave. Draw three **curved lines** for hair, on the side. Add another **line** inside his mouth.

7 Draw two **curved lines** inside his mouth for his tongue.

8 Darken the area inside the mouth.

9 LOOK at the final drawing! Erase extra sketch lines. Add color.

Happy fellow! Happy is always a fun emotion to draw.

Let's draw the same guy again, from a different side, but change his expression. We can do that with just a few simple lines and shapes.

1 Sketch three **ovals** for the head, ear and nose.

2 Draw a small **circle** inside the ear. Add two **ovals** for eyes. Sketch another **oval** for a mouth.

3 Sketch an **oval** overlapping his ear. Draw a wave on the top of his head. Put two small **circles** inside his eyes.

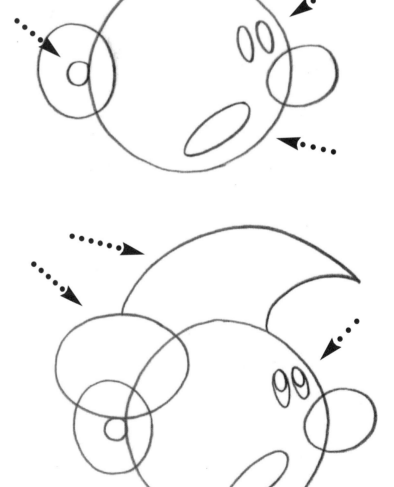

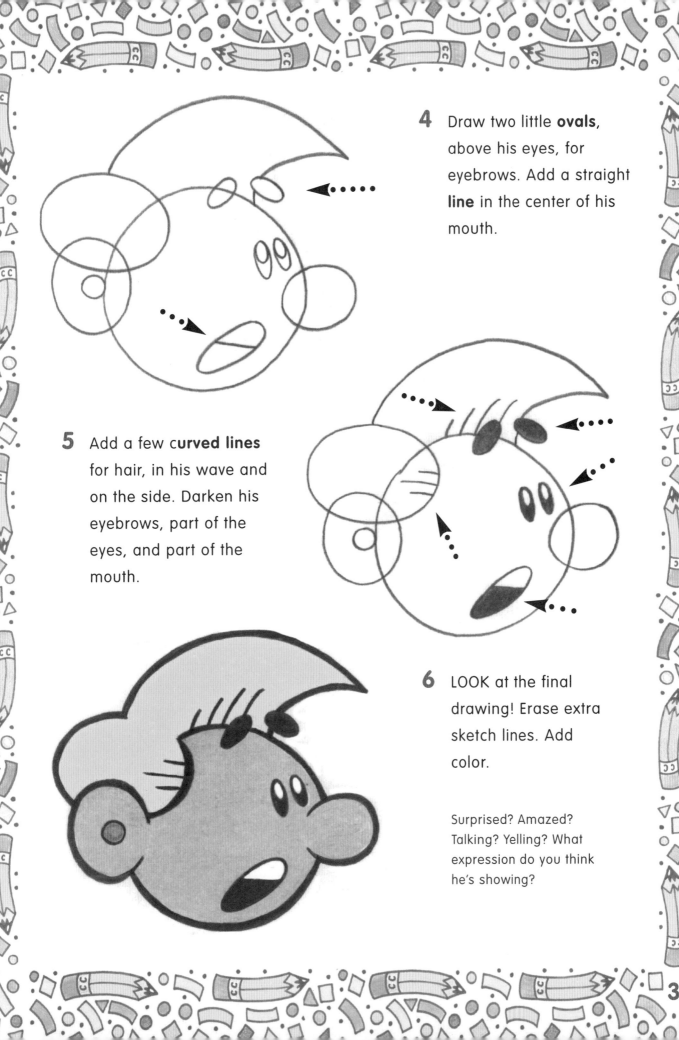

4 Draw two little **ovals**, above his eyes, for eyebrows. Add a straight **line** in the center of his mouth.

5 Add a few **curved lines** for hair, in his wave and on the side. Darken his eyebrows, part of the eyes, and part of the mouth.

6 LOOK at the final drawing! Erase extra sketch lines. Add color.

Surprised? Amazed? Talking? Yelling? What expression do you think he's showing?

With just a few simple lines and shapes, we will change the eyebrows and mouth and make him look really angry.

1   Draw the same basic head. Add a **curved line** for his mouth.

2   Draw two **triangles** for eyebrows. LOOK at the shape of the mouth! Carefully draw two more **curved lines** for the mouth.

3   Darken the eyebrows. Add two **straight lines** to the mouth.

4 Draw a **line** crossing the center line of his mouth. Draw a small **line** next to his mouth to make it look like his jaw muscle is tightening.

5 Add a few **curved lines** around his head to show heat.

6 LOOK at the final drawing! Darken the lines. Add color.

Wow! What a hot head! We'd better try to cheer him up.

Let's draw the same face again, but we'll make him grin from ear to ear.

Look in the mirror and think "really happy." LOOK at your big smile and try to see and feel the shapes your mouth and eyes form.

1 Start with the basic head again.

2 Add two dark **triangles** for eyebrows. Draw a big **curved line** for the top of his mouth.

3 Add two small **curved lines** for his eyes. Draw a big looping **curved line** for the bottom of his mouth.

4 Draw two intersecting **lines** inside his mouth.

5 Sketch a **circle** and two **triangles** for a bow tie.

6 LOOK at the final drawing! Erase extra sketch lines. Add color.

Look at this guy grin! Apparently, he REALLY likes that bow tie you drew for him. You are quite an impressive artist.

Let's add some emotion to a different face.

1   Draw a large **oval** for the head. Add smaller overlapping **ovals** for ear and nose.

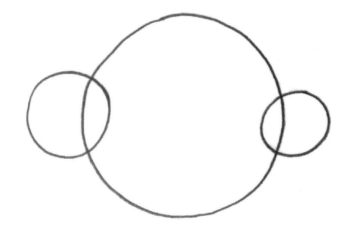

2   Add a small **circle** inside the ear. Draw two large **ovals** for eyes, and a smaller **oval** for the mouth.

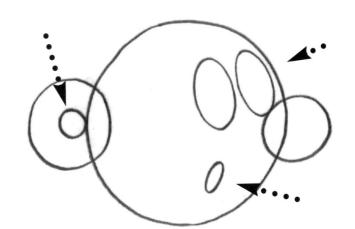

3   Draw two **ovals** inside each eye. Add a **curved line** for hair.

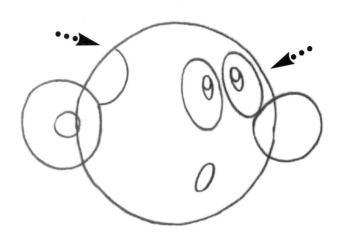

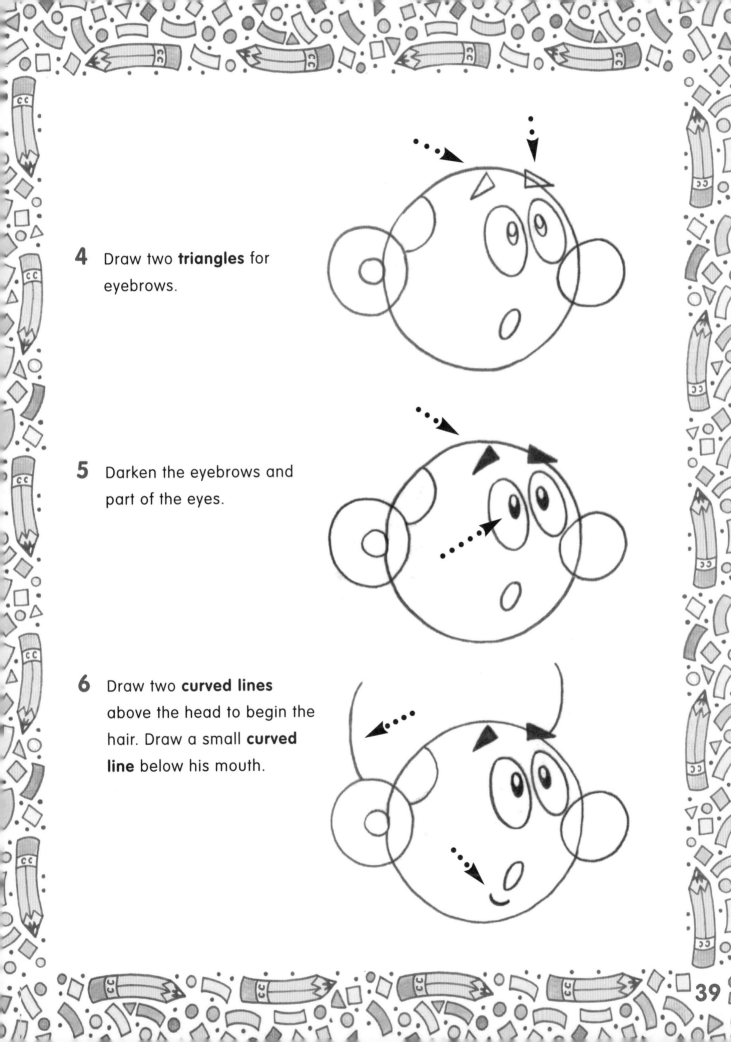

4 Draw two **triangles** for eyebrows.

5 Darken the eyebrows and part of the eyes.

6 Draw two **curved lines** above the head to begin the hair. Draw a small **curved line** below his mouth.

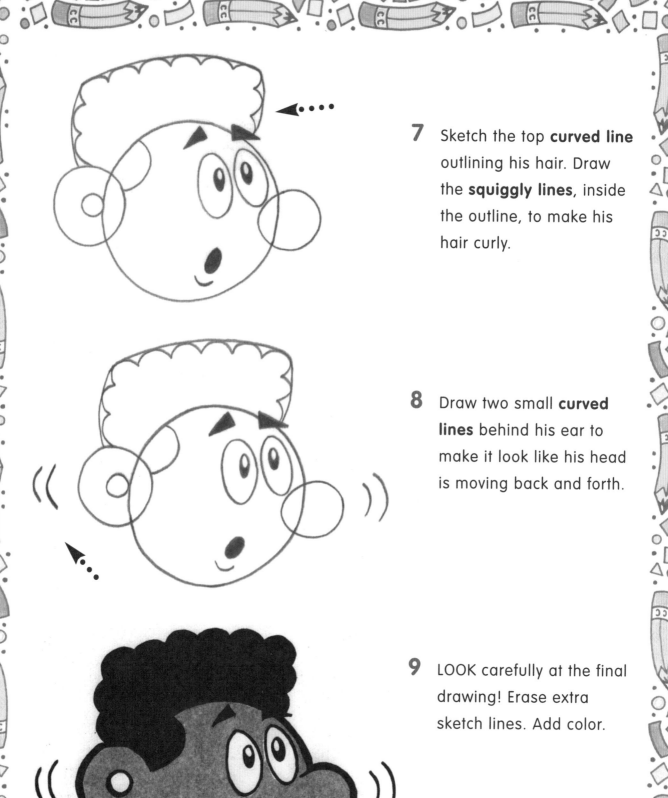

7 Sketch the top **curved line** outlining his hair. Draw the **squiggly lines**, inside the outline, to make his hair curly.

8 Draw two small **curved lines** behind his ear to make it look like his head is moving back and forth.

9 LOOK carefully at the final drawing! Erase extra sketch lines. Add color.

He sure looks surprised.

Great job!

Glasses

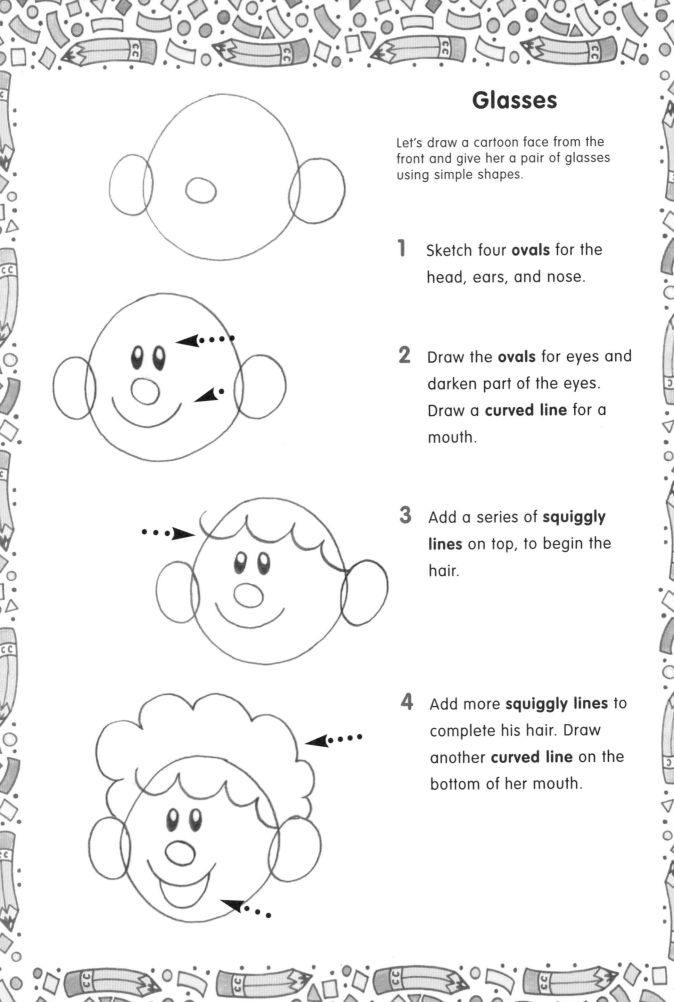

Let's draw a cartoon face from the front and give her a pair of glasses using simple shapes.

1 Sketch four **ovals** for the head, ears, and nose.

2 Draw the **ovals** for eyes and darken part of the eyes. Draw a **curved line** for a mouth.

3 Add a series of **squiggly lines** on top, to begin the hair.

4 Add more **squiggly lines** to complete his hair. Draw another **curved line** on the bottom of her mouth.

5 Draw a small **curved line** on the end of her mouth to make a cheek. Add a **curved line** in the center of her mouth.

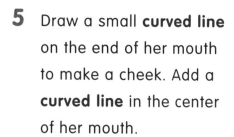

6 Draw two **circles** and three **straight lines** to make her glasses. Darken part of the mouth.

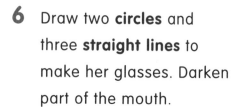

7 LOOK at the final drawing! Erase extra sketch lines. Add color.

Good job!

Look closely at these examples of glasses. Can you see what shapes and lines are used to make them?

Draw them!

Next time you are at the mall or out in public somewhere, look at people's glasses and try to see what shapes they are made from.

When you get home, draw a cartoon face with some of the things you have seen.

Hats

Hats say a great deal about the people wearing them.

You can make hats with all sorts of unusual shapes and combinations of lines. Let's try drawing a few simple hats now. Later you can experiment with different lines and shapes to create your own hats.

Let's start with a baseball cap.

1   Sketch a large **oval** for the head, and a smaller one for the nose.

2   Draw **ovals** for eyes. Draw a long, thin **oval** on top to begin her cap. Sketch a **circle** for hair, on the side. Draw a **curved line** for her mouth.

3   Sketch two **circles** to begin her pigtail. Darken part of her eyes.

4   Add a large **curved line** on top to finish the cap shape. Draw a small **curved line** on each side of her mouth.

5 Sketch a small **circle** on top of her hat, and add two **curved lines** to give it seams. Draw an upside-down tear shape to complete her pigtail.

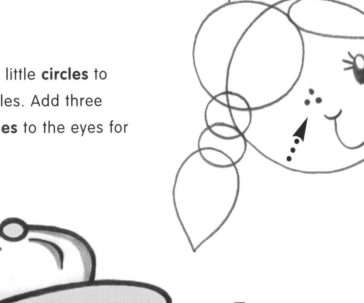

6 Draw three little **circles** to make freckles. Add three **straight lines** to the eyes for eyelashes.

7 LOOK at the final drawing! Erase extra sketch lines. Add color.

She looks like a real champ. You are an amazing artist.

Now, let's draw a colorful top hat.

1 Sketch three overlapping **ovals**, for the head, ear, and nose.

2 Draw a **circle** inside the ear. Draw two **straight lines** for eyebrows. Add two **ovals** under them for eyes.

3 Draw a small **oval** inside each eye. Add two **curved lines** for a smiling mouth.

4 Sketch an **oval** above his ear for hair. Add two **curved lines** above his eyebrows. Darken part of the eyes.

5 Draw four **straight lines** to begin his top hat.

6 Draw a **straight line** across the top of the hat. Add a **curved line** in the middle. Draw **curved lines** to finish the hat's brim.

7 Erase extra sketch lines. Darken final lines. Add color.

Terrific top hat!

Some hats can be drawn with just a few lines. Let me show you a fun wizard's hat to draw.

1 Sketch a large **oval** for the head, with two smaller overlapping **ovals** for the ear and nose.

2 Sketch an **oval** on the left side for hair. Draw a **circle** inside the ear. Draw **ovals** for the eyes. Darken part of the eyes.

3 Add a wave for his hair. Draw two **curved lines** to make the mouth.

4 Draw two **curved lines** for his eyebrows.

5 Draw **curved lines** for the bottoms of the eyebrows. Draw an upside-down wave below his chin.

6 Sketch two **ovals** under his nose for a moustache.

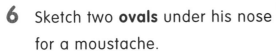

7 LOOK carefully at the final drawing! Draw a **triangle** for the hat. Add a few stars or circles to his hat. Add color.

Cool cartoon wizard!

Here's one more simple hat to draw.

1 Sketch three **ovals** again.

2 Draw an **oval**, inside an **oval**, for his eye. Draw two **curved lines** for a smile.

3 Draw a **curved line** and a **straight line** on top of his head for his hat. Darken part of the eye, and draw a big **oval** around it.

4 Add a **straight line** to the middle of his hat. Draw a **straight line** for his glasses.

5 LOOK at the final drawing! erase extra sketch lines. Add color.

Way to go! Delightful derby! You drew great glasses too.

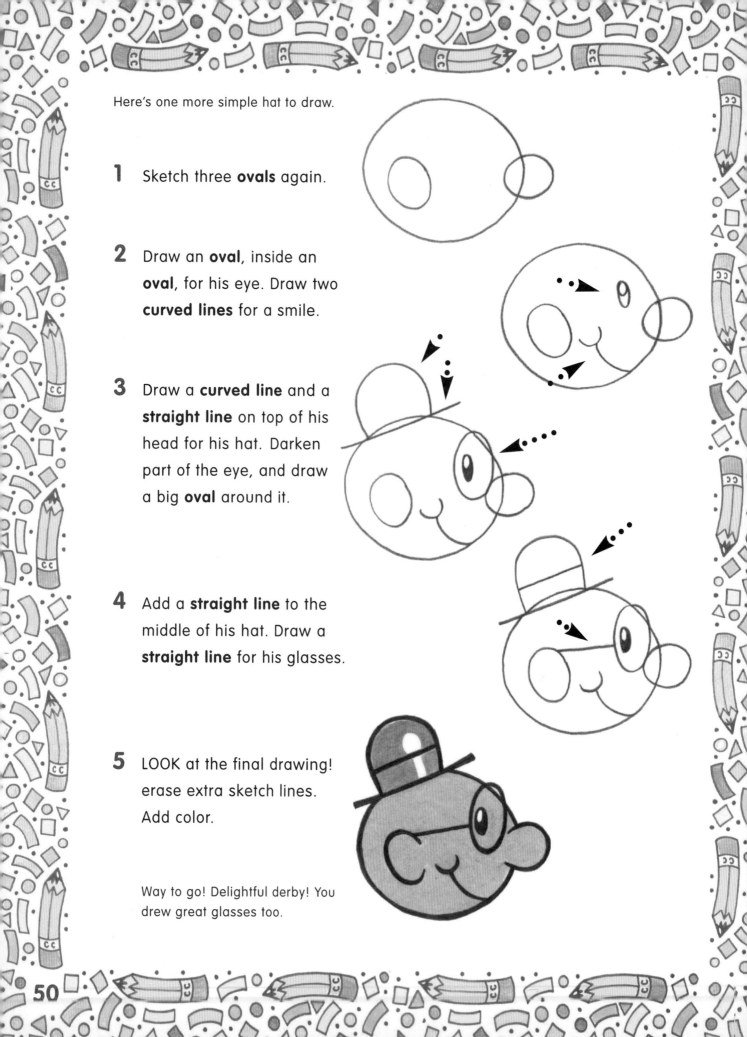

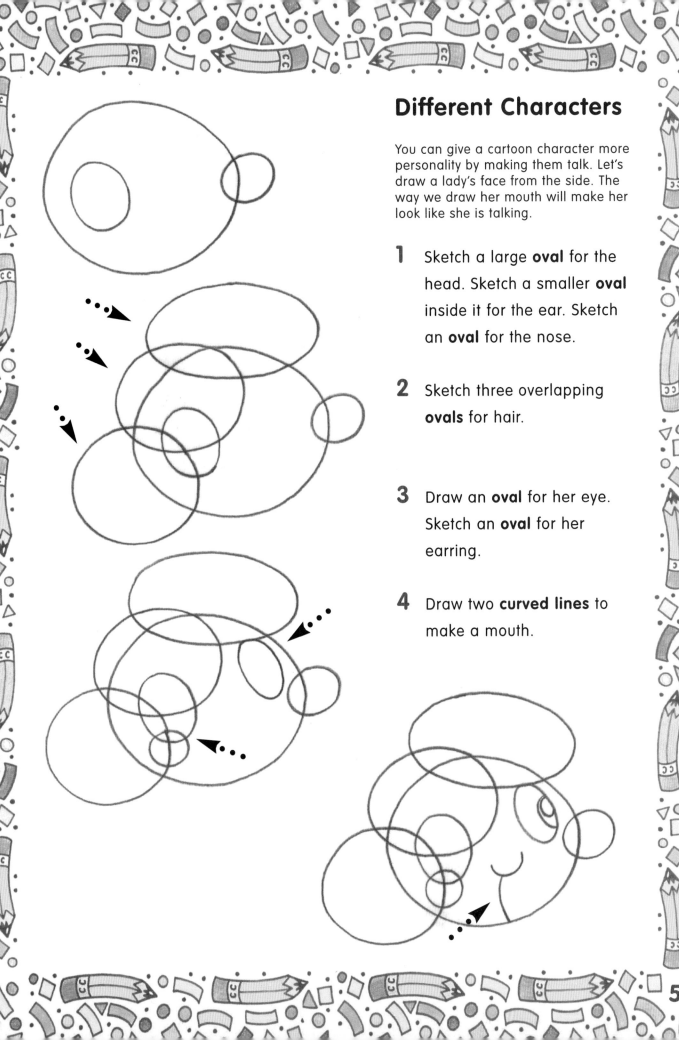

Different Characters

You can give a cartoon character more personality by making them talk. Let's draw a lady's face from the side. The way we draw her mouth will make her look like she is talking.

1 Sketch a large **oval** for the head. Sketch a smaller **oval** inside it for the ear. Sketch an **oval** for the nose.

2 Sketch three overlapping **ovals** for hair.

3 Draw an **oval** for her eye. Sketch an **oval** for her earring.

4 Draw two **curved lines** to make a mouth.

5 Draw three short **lines** for eyelashes. Draw another **curved line** for her mouth.

6 Add a few **curved lines** to give her hair a little texture. Darken part of the eye.

7 LOOK at the final drawing! Erase extra sketch lines. Add color.

Wow! She is talking!

Good job!

It is time for grandmother to take a little nap. Let's take this opportunity to learn how to draw a sleeping cartoon character.

1 Sketch a large **oval** for her head. Sketch two smaller **ovals** for her ear and nose.

2 Sketch two large **ovals** for hair. Draw two small **curved lines** for her eyes.

3 Sketch another **oval** for more hair. Draw a tiny **oval** to make a great cartoon mouth.

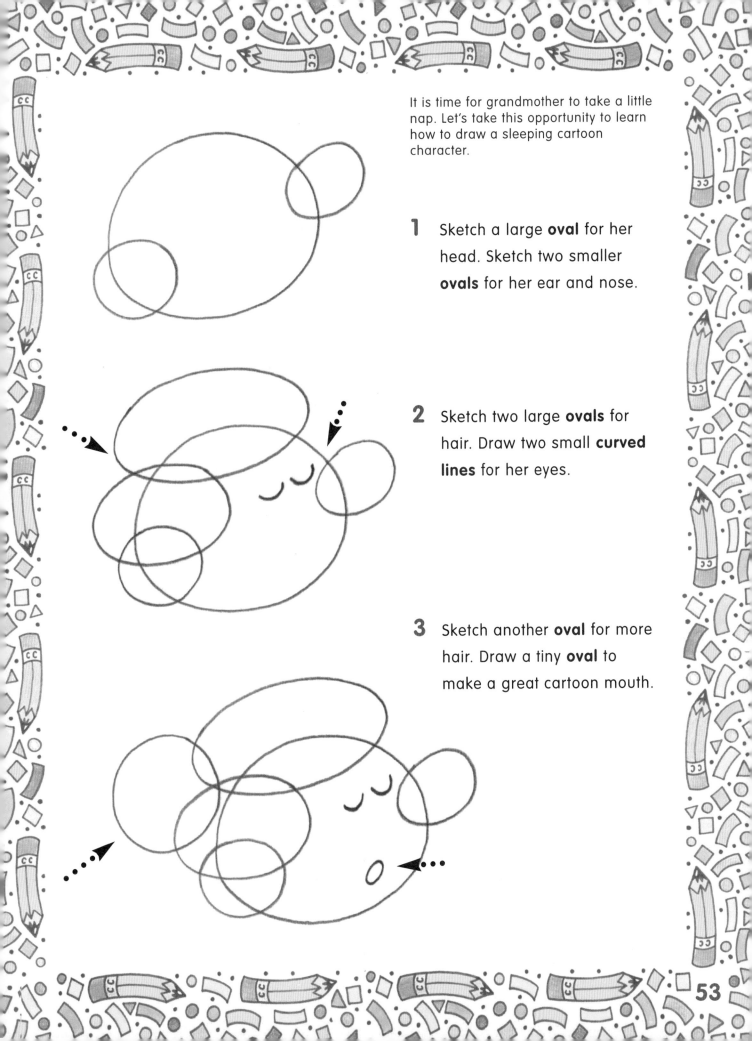

4 Add **curved lines** to her hair. Draw three **straight lines** on each eye for eyelashes.

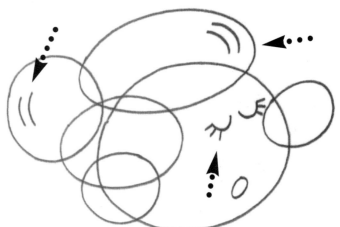

5 Draw some "Zs" around her mouth and nose. Darken her mouth.

6 LOOK at the final drawing! Erase extra sketch lines. Add color.

The Zs are the cartoonist's way of showing the character is snoring. Grandmother sure is snoozing. Let's try to draw the next exercise quietly so we don't wake her up!

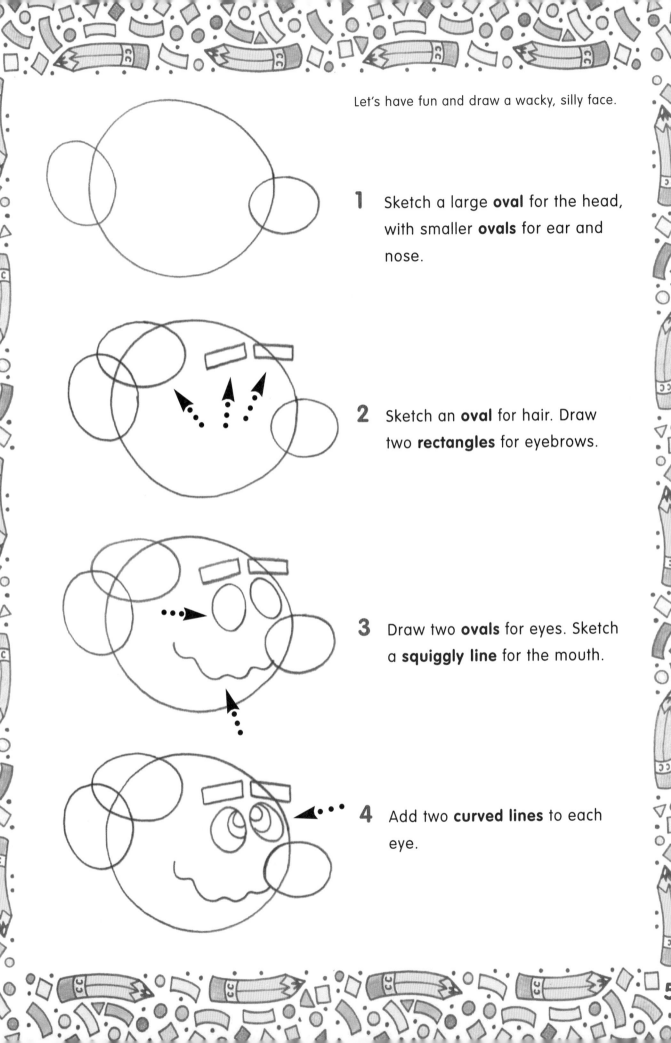

Let's have fun and draw a wacky, silly face.

1 Sketch a large **oval** for the head, with smaller **ovals** for ear and nose.

2 Sketch an **oval** for hair. Draw two **rectangles** for eyebrows.

3 Draw two **ovals** for eyes. Sketch a **squiggly line** for the mouth.

4 Add two **curved lines** to each eye.

5 Draw a **curved line** and a **straight line** under the mouth for his tongue.

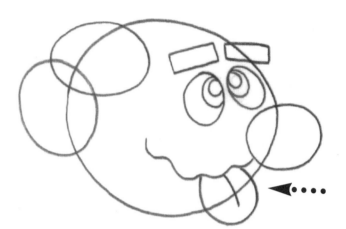

6 Darken his eyebrows and part of his eyes. Add a small **curved line** at the corner of his mouth.

8 LOOK at the final drawing! Erase extra sketch lines. Add color.

What a silly face! I bet his mom told him when he was little to stop making that face or it would freeze like that, and he didn't listen to her!

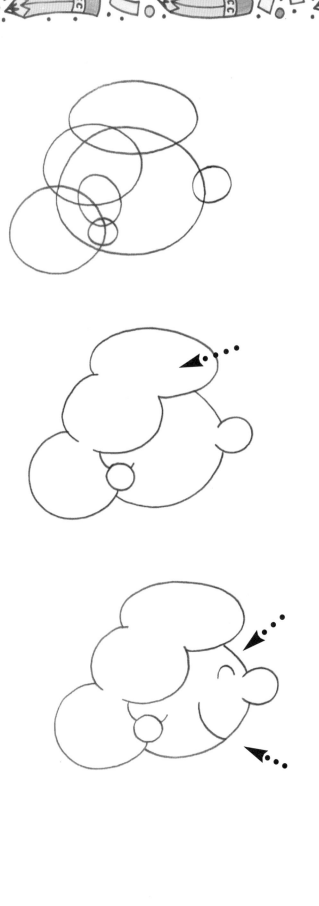

You can alter a character's expression dramatically by changing simple lines on the mouth and eyes. Let's draw the lady's face again without an eye or mouth.

1 Sketch the head, nose, hair, ear and earring **ovals** again.

2 Erase extra sketch lines. Darken the final lines.

3 Draw a simple **curved line** for her eyebrow. Add a **curved line** for her mouth. She is very happy.

4 Draw the **curved lines** upside down. She is not a happy camper anymore.

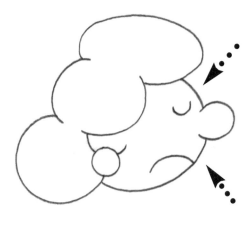

Triangles, Squares, and Rectangles

To make a cartoon character's face look more like an alien or a robot, you can use triangles, squares, or rectangles. Let's draw a cartoon character's face using a triangle.

1   Sketch a **triangle** for the head.

2   Add two small **triangles** for eyebrows. Draw a **circle** for the nose. Add two **curved lines** for the ears.

3   Draw the **squiggly lines** for hair. Draw the eyes, mouth, and round neck. Add a **straight line** to each ear.

4   LOOK at the final drawing! Darken final lines. Add color.

Let's have a little fun and draw a really square face.

1 Sketch a **square** for the head. Draw an **oval** for the nose. Add the **curved lines** for the mouth.

2 Draw two **ovals** for eyebrows. Draw two **straight lines** for each eye.

3. Draw **squiggly lines** for hair. Draw **curved lines** for his ears.

4 LOOK at the final drawing! Darken final lines. Add color.

You have learned a lot about cartooning in this book. By now, you should be able to draw a cool cartoon character just by carefully looking at the shapes and lines you see.

1-2-3, draw the shapes and lines you see!

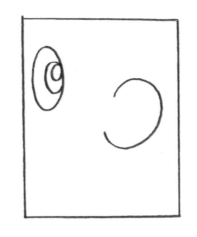

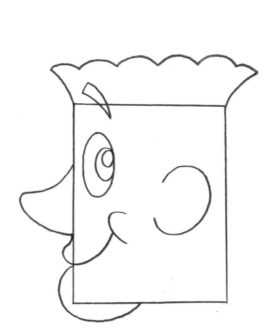

Practice, practice, practice!

Have fun creating your own unique characters. Maybe you will end up creating the most popular cartoon character in the history of the world. If you do, please remember to invite me to your amusement park!

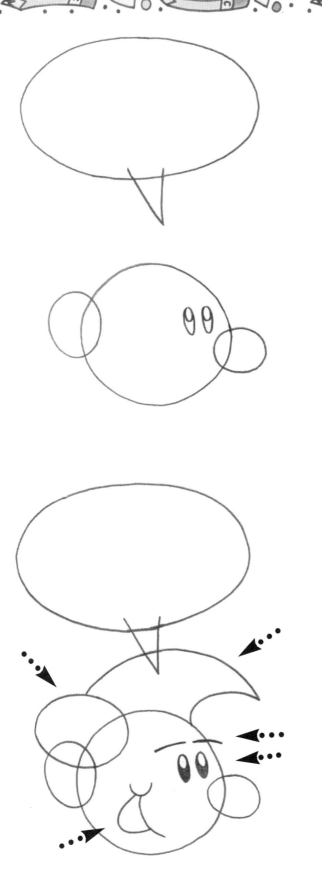

Talking Characters

Printed cartoon characters talk using something called a word balloon. It is a sort of bubble that appears over the character's head. It makes it seem like the character is speaking. Let's draw a cartoon character talking.

1 Sketch a large **oval** for the word balloon. Add two **lines**. Sketch **ovals** for the head, ear, nose, and eyes under it.

2 Sketch an **oval** and a wave shape for hair. Draw two **lines** to begin the eyebrows. Darken part of the eyes. Draw three **curved lines** to make a mouth.

3 Draw three **straight lines** for hair strands. Add **curved lines** to complete the eyebrows.

4 LOOK at the final drawing! Erase extra sketch lines. Draw words inside the word balloon. You can make your character say whatever you wish. Add color.

GREAT JOB! You are officially trained to draw cartoon faces. Congratulations!

Award yourself! On the next page you'll find an award certificate you can photocopy to let the world know you're a **Cartoonist's Apprentice First Class!**

Have you enjoyed this book?

Find out about other books in this series and see sample pages online at

www.123draw.com